PUNKY WEIRDO

Canada's new

punk poet

Cyberwit.net
HIG 45 Kaushambi Kunj, Kalindipuram
Allahabad - 211011 (U.P.) India
http://www.cyberwit.net

Tel: +(91) 9415091004 +(91) (532) 2552257

E-mail: info@cyberwit.net

Printed at Repro India Limited.

FOR KELLY ERIN DUFFY, THE PRETTIEST GIRL EVER

Contents

Hard Times 7
I Am Tomorrow 8
Cat 10
Unity I 11
The Moon is on Fire 12
Smile 13
Perfect Town 14
Dusty Underground Palace 15
Yellow Light 16
Shiverin Pete 17
The Geek 18
The Meek 19
Chin 20
Tomorrow Morning 21
Troll 22
The Other Side 23
Leave it on The Stage 24
Hades Monocle 25
The Oblivious Procrastinator 26
Hades Monocle 2 27
Confused 28
All Things Wired 29
Not Me 30
Backwards 31
Nothing 32
Search the Sky 33
Bad Place 34
Gotta Get Home 35
Laws 37
The Turkey 38
This Pen Sucks 39

Driven by Sloth 40

Looking for Crazy 43

It's Cold 44

Cocaine 45

Let's Go Drinking 46

For You 47

Unity II 48

Box of Pine 49

All Together Ever More 50

Music 51

Stupid Get Angry 52

Guilt 53

Transmissions 54

Consume 55

New Clown in Town 56

After The End 58

Skeletons 59

Mainstream 60

Lost 61

Individuals 62

Anger 63

Religion 64

Dementia 65

Doomed 66

Temptation 67

One Hell of a Storm 68

Salvation 69

Succeed 70

Pride 71

Drunk 72

Mars 73

The Last 74

Temptation II 75

Distress 76

Dusty Underground Palace II 77

Peace 78
Numb 79
Unheard 80
Generation Gap 81
Goodbye 82
Approaching the End 83
The last one in the book 84

Hard Times

To me it seems there's a new need
To feed the brain
There are people in trouble
They were left out in the rain
They were misunderstood
They were condemned from the start
Characterized for their dysfunctional minds
And not their true beating hearts
Suffer the poet
The poppies grow
The sun comes up
The curtains close

I Am Tomorrow

I am tomorrow I am what they all said

I am financial collapse

I am streets running red

I am dirty needle

I am rotting fruit

I am ten dollar sneaker

I am ten thousand dollar suit

I am tomorrow

I am a kick in the head

I am steal before borrow

I am prayer before bed

I am abandoned infant

I am vanishing trees

I am hate for the masses

I am rising of seas

I am tomorrow

I am the wrong note

I am enemy to harmony

I am friends with the Pope

I am everything to lose

I am sulfur breeze

I am forever grey

I am spreading disease

I am tomorrow

I am lined up to feed

I am gold but transparent

I am the product of greed

I am the last common thread
I am perfect storm
I am some dismal future
And you have all been warned

Cat

I am a cat
I am completely useless
I am genetically stupid
But I can kill rats
How 'bout that
And I can kill mice
The big people don't think it's nice
When I leave 'em at the back door
No one knows what for
It's not because I'm proud
Rational thought is not allowed
Cuz I'm a cat
How 'bout that I am a cat
And I'll piss on your clothes if I don't get my way
I eat so much I puke but I keep eating all the same
Because I am a cat as a matter of fact
And I'll beg you to pet me but I'll bite you
And I'll sleep on your head because I believe I have the right to
Because I am a cat
How about that!

Unity I

Reality is a nightmare
Religion is a war
Faith and hope are deadbolt locks
Decision is a door
The system is a dropout
The planet is a site
The countryside's a memory
The family is a fight
Education is a job
A compliment's a blow
Hedonism is majority
Redemption is a glow
Honesty is old school
History is pain
Politicians are enemies
Society is a drain
Acceptance is gold
Privacy is grey
Prejudice is lost
Unity is the way

The Moon is on Fire

They remain quiet when they don't believe it
They don't believe because they never win
They never win because they're unprepared
They're unprepared because they're always late
They're always late because they have no time
They have no time because they're on the run
They're on the run because they forgot how to walk
They forgot how to walk because they're caught up in a race
They're caught up in a race because they've been told to win
They've been told to win by those who have lost
Those who have lost want another chance
When chance arrives the losers are sleeping
The losers are sleeping cuz they're tired of losing
And when they're not losing they're obviously cheating
They cheat because the moon is on fire
The moon is on fire because there's no oxygen in space
Actually there is but it's very expensive
It's very expensive because the cows have stopped laughing
The cows have stopped laughing because the pigs have stole
their weed
The pigs steal everybody's weed but that's another story

Smile

He's got nothing
At least he's got that
He could turn it into something
If he could pass around a hat
A hat would really be something
Expressionless for a while
He doesn't have a hat to pass around
So he begins to pass around a smile

Perfect Town

It was a boring day, down at the lake
We were just driving around
When we followed a shiny golden arrow
And ended up in Perfect Town
We could tell as soon as we showed up, showing off was what
was going down
We could tell by the looks on their faces they didn't want people
like us being around
Cuz you gotta be perfect in Perfect Town
Doin' what's right was going around
But they were all selfish self-righteous clowns
So we decided to burn down Perfect Town
And now Perfect Town ain't perfect no more
The mob came calling looking to score
Those perfect people lost their dream
And now they are forced to learn to live without greed

Dusty Underground Palace

Dues have been paid the standing have been counted
They've planned a parade and the horses are mounted
Tears falling from windows
No one offering to lead
It's easier this way no one has to concede
Cuz we are the only ones
Who can change the light bulbs on the sun
You trample on us anyway
Because we live up in the sky
You laugh at us and wonder why
We know most of you will not see better days
We'll show you the end and make sure you have fun
We live by the pen but die by the gun
Tears falling in the gutter
Marching past with fiendish grin
We know why they gave in
We know just where they've been
And below them the faintest rumbling sound
From a palace in the dusty underground
Confusion being created by the brave
You trample on us anyway
Changing light bulbs on the sun
Makes things bright for everyone

Yellow Light

There's a slow man crossing on a yellow light
The streets are quiet and empty
But it's a dark and foggy night

Shiverin Pete

Shiverin Pete has been left all alone
He woke up in the dark and there's nobody home
How will he manage his first thought on his own
Shiverin Pete can't pick up the phone
Where has everyone gone
Why did they forget me
Why are there no lights on
The world it seems has abandoned me
But I have done nothing wrong
So I pace the halls and pray to the unknown
I cry in the middle of the night
I am terrified of what's to come
Because I have no comfort in sight
But exhausted from this fear I collapse
Hoping someone will come to my call
I hope they find me before my doom
But there is no answer at all

{Petey was a friend's dog I once took care of while he was away, the poor dog howled all night}

The Geek

Suckin on an icecube
Four fans pointed at me
Thinking about importing snow
Praying for a cool breeze
My eyeballs are sweating
Feet dangle in the pool
Water's just about to boil
Why can't I be cool?

The Meek

How did they get here
Here being nowhere
Who or what made them wrong
Just look at them they don't seem right
Even the ones with natural eyes
As opposed to the ones screwed into their heads
Some turn yellow, most are always red
Displaced families, children will lose their way
In the back of parked cars, they waste their days
The free market economy hands out sleeping bags at Christmas
Raise your hand if you don't mind the rain
It doesn't make sense
They can't all be insane
They can't all be on drugs
Unwanted thugs
From early broken homes
Mom went to the store and left us alone… Forever
And never knowing why makes forever a long time
Hard to walk a straight line
Mental condition incurable disease
Defeat the odds or die in the street
Just can't afford that first and last
The reason they try to forget the past
Their future decided between their conception and birth
Society decays and they inherit the earth

Chin

I used to have a chin
And a perfectly shaped grin
People wondered where I'd been
But then I lost my chin while I was out for a spin.
Has anybody seen my chin?
I checked the lost & found
It keeps falling off my face
And it feels like it weighs about a million pounds
It's actually weighed in kilos, but I don't know how to convert
Every time I lose it my bottom lip hangs down
And I drool all over my shirt
I think my chin left town
It disappeared into a crowd
I yelled "I really need you" loud
You're the only one that can support my jowls
Pardon me have you seen my chin
He smells like smoke an drinks lots of gin
He won't come back 'til I give in
And admit that I belong to him

Tomorrow Morning

Tomorrow morning, I will change my evil ways
Tomorrow morning, I will make plans for better days
Tomorrow morning, I will worry about the grey
Tomorrow morning, I will straighten up and fly right
But not today

Troll

Hideous, deformed, grotesque
Down low, bottom, under
Hidden gutter, sunken, covered
Dark, empty, silent, cold
Hunger, torture, panic
Troll, troll, troll
I say he's a big mean green fucker, stay out of his way
Shadows, echoes, voices still
Followed, watching, waiting, kill
Slaughter, devour, rejoice, behold
Severed heads dinner
Troll, troll, troll
I tell you
Cuz he's mean and he's green
And he's full of rage
He's a real mother fucker
So just stay out of his way

The Other Side

The other side is horrifying
Far worse than you would believe
Far worse than any hellish landscape
That you've ever imagined or seen
We go to reality when we die
There's only hard labour on the other side
There is no rest, it's what you don't want
The white light deceives, we've been doomed all along
Trust me, you don't want to die
There's empty sadness on the other side
There are politics in the cosmic scheme
Living a psychotically ever-changing bad dream

Leave it on The Stage

Hey old friend what troubles you
Does your torment have a name
Some shocking event that's left you disturbed
Were you stepped on along the way
You can open up and talk about it
How have they kept you maintained
Without opening up this unhealing wound
Please tell me just what caused the change
Or have you bought into an illusion
Is your damage what we should expect
Fully aware of the psychosis
And somehow still demand respect
Hostility, frustration, anxiety and rage
Leave it all behind you
Leave it on the stage

Hades Monocle

Grey water tide pools and hot sulfur springs
Magnify the future
What woe the beast will bring
A view into eternity
A purpose of temptation
A race against reality
Will you see me off at the station?
Molecular propulsion cannot help me
But I know where the question ends
You only have to see through it once
There's a truth that cannot bend
Reach into the vision
A reason to alter the landscape
Concentrate on every intention
And preview the choices you'll soon have to make
Scorched earth through baron fields
Torn flesh survival
The slaughter never yields
And yet you had to see it for yourself
You're a prophet now, you have stories to tell
But ultimately you'll follow me into hell.
The view to the kill
Pulling out of the station
It's the very last train
One more sonic vibration.

The Oblivious Procrastinator

I don't want to look back into the thing that watches me
Possessed by the darkness
The blackened abyss for all to see
For I am the oblivious procrastinator
And I have travelled infinitely
Set free on the onset of creation
As a result of the cosmic scheme
Hesitation, even creation itself could have happened sooner
All things are incapable of perpetual immediate reaction
We just cannot constantly initiate
A tree in the wind bends to one side
The branches prepare just as the wind dies
Why is it hesitation we see?
The branches know exactly where they're supposed to be
My existence is pondering and I know not why
I will never know but I will still look for the reason
So as conscious life joined our existence long ago
I made sure the most intelligent life was infected with inconsistency, doubt, hesitation and procrastination
But I know not why
I am unaware of the reason
All things wait
Even if for just a second
From the day the sun first shone
To the man who invented the yellow light.

Hades Monocle 2

A giant hand
A giant magnifying glass
Magnifying a tiny little bomb
An obstruction of view
A looking glass to look through
It's been watching us all along

Confused

I can't seem to find anything to go
And I can't find anywhere to do
My shoes are on the ceiling
The front door is out back
And the basement is on the roof
I'm so confused
Cuz the mailman's delivering pizza
And the cat's chasing the dog
The moon came up this morning
And the news says nothing wrong
And I just don't see what they say
And you never hear how they move
While we waste away hiding out in plain sight
While we prove there is nothing to prove.

All Things Wired

I can't imagine doing this without it

It's change for the jukebox

The landscape that inspires

Its imagination unlocked

The collective collectively wired

Your soul just gets in the way

And you may have to fight to get it back someday

The chords that tangle their way across the floor

Have a purpose for keeping balance

When creating a score

Anger and purpose

Regret and ambition

Building a building

Forever my mission

Interstellar architect

When guessing the answer's always correct

Not Me

I Didn't Do It
I was not he who was responsible
It was not me
I was nowhere near it
No I was not there
I knew not of it
I was totally unaware
I am completely innocent
I am free of guilt
And I will stand firm against the case you have built
I've got a pocket full of alibis
And I see clearly through the lies
I don't care what their argument was
I don't know what they're fighting for
I refuse to be summoned into this battle
I will not fight someone else's war

Backwards

The idea burns and turns to ash
Ignites the soul, the minutes pass
Grab ahold it will slip through your grasp
Gift or curse it becomes the past
The process is original I have taken a different path
Creatively upside down and in reverse
First things last
And last things first

Nothing

Nothing knows exactly what everything is
While everything has no idea
And wants nothing to do with nothing

Search the Sky

Search the sky, it's worth it
From my heart to my soul
From my pen to the page
From my mind to my fingers
From these words to the stage
I can will it to happen
I speak from the hip
And when I get it wrong
I abandon the ship

Search the sky, it's worth it

The best of the arts
The strange, the free
True and angry
Brave and extreme
Suffer the curse – Frustration
Struggle with articulation
How can they teach you when you don't listen
And ignorant bliss never knows what it's missing

Bad Place

I'm falling apart
I'm out of the race
I am full of pain
I am in a bad place

I've been robbed of time
I have fallen from grace
I chose the wrong path
And now I'm in a bad place

I have wasted my days
I joined the wrong chase
I fought a losing fight
And I'm in a bad place

But I won't resign from the struggle
In order to save face
Cause everyone every once in a while
Finds themselves in a bad place

Gotta Get Home

I can't drink anymore
Did too many drugs
Gotta call a taxi
Starting to see double
I want to pass out
But I gotta get home
Or have one more beer
Do some more drugs
No I gotta go home
I can't see straight
Where are my smokes
A big pile of shoes
My jacket's downstairs
That couch is starting to look good
Maybe crash here
No I gotta get home
She don't know where I am
I didn't even phone
She's gunna be pissed I gotta get home
My paycheque is gone
Has it been three days?
I'm probably locked out
Maybe I should stay
So someone roll a joint
Or chop me a line
Pass me a beer
Help me think up a lie
The couch calls my name

Toothpicks in my eyes
That poker game was fixed
Help me think of a lie
I'm totally fucked
No point going home
I've done her wrong again
I'm going to end up alone
But... by chance I check my messages
To my surprise
I couldn't believe my luck
She said hope you didn't get too fucked up this weekend
And if you blew your pay I can lend you a few bucks

Laws

So I told the privileged my beliefs
I told them I had been a thief
But that I had never stole from thieves
I told them that I followed no laws
And that all religions were full of flaws
And I rely on the youth to plot discourse
And change old ways by choice not force

The Turkey

The turkey couldn't gobble, he was gibbled
The bottle had been passed he drank a little
But then he drank some more
And soon passed out on the floor
So the turkey couldn't gobble, he was gibbled

They got him to his feet
He stood and wobbled
He tried to talk he just drooled and driveled
So to the bar he hobbled
And he polished off that bottle
And the turkey couldn't gobble, he was gibbled

This Pen Sucks

This pen sucks
Is this pen gonna work!
Oh it seems ok now

But maybe I should go find another one
It didn't feel right when I first started out

And there that last line was faint
Maybe I should just go get my paint

Then paint a picture of a pen
One that writes really smooth

But then again the shitty pen was good enough for this poem
I guess I ain't got nothing to lose

This poem was written with one shitty pen
Just go ask Bob Dylan, it happens now and then

And so one last verse, before I go search
For a better writing utensil
A marker, crayon, paint brush or pastel
A piece of chalk or pencil

Driven by Sloth

How many more dues am I expected to pay?
I do not have to be turned, I can lead myself astray

Never sure what my intentions are
And my attention span is shot to hell
But I would not want it any other way
I try not to know myself too well

I am completely irresponsible
I argue and I swear
And you can only have a piece of me
Because I am not all there

I know where I've gone wrong
I won't let myself forget
But I will not dwell on my past too long
I refuse to have regrets

Just what line do you want me to stand in?
Tell me the secret and give me understanding

I once moved a mountain
And then I climbed up top
I'm standing on a ledge overlooking the edge
Thinking about the drop

I've been sitting on a fence
Now and then I jump off

But I keep switching sides
I can't make up my mind
Just what side I should be on

My history is of puzzles and games
But it's Tug of War I most often play
Maybe I'll never reap salvation
But the challenge won't go away

I dig holes and I sit on fences
And I often do things that heighten my senses
I've been robbed by the rich
I try not to cry poor
But I don't want to be trapped inside this game anymore

I've left a reminder to jump through the next window
Hoping it leads to the end of the rainbow

I'm digging a hole, leaving a dent
Alone in the field sitting on my fence
The mountain I move the mountain I climb
The windows I miss, too far or too high

This hole that I dig helps me find the things that float around my room
The invisible wiggly lines
That breathe and come alive
Heard but unseen and understood by very few
So just where would you want to be
Climbing the ladder to the high life
Or stuck down in the hole with me

Don't kid yourself, we may not be leaving
Everyone down here tries to climb out
A spark of inspiration makes for believing
But the comfort of my future will not be in doubt

Lost faith turns to oncoming madness
But I'm sure that it won't last
I will get served what I deserve
But the future will eventually pass

But you probably think that you now know me well
Don't get too close I'll lead you straight to hell
Don't follow my ways don't live as I do
There are too many obstacles I have to fight through

So tell me who really cares
Somebody please raise a hand
Drop the game you've been playing and follow along
And listen to me I have changed my plans

The truth is I always want comfort
I always want to feel good
But I don't always want to do the things that I know I should

So listen close do you understand, I found myself in desperate need
Would prosperity still escape me had I been driven by greed
And not sloth?

Looking for Crazy

I've been looking for crazy
Cuz I've been told that's where it's at

I'd like to wander alone
Down foreign cobblestone roads
Crazy will be where I hang my hat

I've done everything that I can
To slow down the ever grinding idea wheel
I know that most wouldn't understand
They lie to themselves and say they know how it feels

So I thought up something positive
To go against my grain
There was laughter but no happiness
There was thunder but no rain

So I walk through the woods
And I speak with the trees
They understand how I feel
I had to think of the positive
For my reality isn't real

Maybe with the right kind of psychotropic help
I might just find my way home
For my sanity is maddening and the game is a hoax
May I return to find the normal unknown

It's Cold

I started at the north end of my street
And started my journey south
I had acquired intolerance to the winter freeze
So I just burned down my house

Then I burned down the rest of my block
I hope no one got killed
Cuz I'm gonna set this city on fire tonight
To fight December's chill

Born up here in the great white north
Born to freeze in the snow
I'm the great Canadian pyro baby
Because I really hate being cold

Cocaine

Who's got the cocaine
It's time for me to freeze my brain
For hours on end I will explain
While my money goes down the drain

Let's Go Drinking

A beautiful day sun is shining
Fuck work I say let's go drinking
Bright and gleaming
And I begin scheming
I'm not going in let's go drinking
The good weather is here let's get a keg of beer
I am calling in sick lets' go drinking
I'm taking today off
Boss knows what I'm thinking
Sun keeps shining
Fuck work let's go drinking

For You

In times that I am not with you
I will be somewhere thinking of you
You surround me I can't wander very far

I'd like to give you something back
So I pulled these words out of a hat
A poem for you, you know just who you are

Not just for not disposing of me
Not just for the tolerated lunacy
You're always just a call away
Although you might not want to hear what I have to say

There may be times that I am away for a while
I'll be on the late train wasting the miles
Searching for things that might not be there
Forever I will continue to look
For proof that I care

Unity II

Disdain and vitriol
Is this system of society
Pure disregard towards those with authority

This old heart still beats with youthful ferocity
And though I am grey and out of touch
I still believe in unity

Box of Pine

The postman just departed, he was blind
His bone white hand handed me a piece of paper and I signed
No return address just a six foot box of pine

So I opened it up, got in and laid down
That box of pine fits fine
Somewhere down the line I'm going to need that box of pine

Later on that night I dug a hole 6 feet deep
Threw in the box, jumped in, laid down and proceeded to fall asleep
When I woke up the next morning I had to dig myself out
Is someone trying to bury me or is this just a sign of doubt

So I guess the moral to the story of the six foot box of pine
Is never make plans for things to go bad
We can worry about things when we die

All Together Ever More

Completely in trance
As I appeared before
The exalted high professors
Of all together ever more

I said I have a complaint
All these different religions seem a constricting restraint
So if you are so old and wise
Tell me why our past is based on lies
What do I need learn
With whom shall I speak
Why do so many still believe
Faith will overcome grief, prayers cure the sick
And any proof of the otherwise is just the devil doing his tricks

Music

Tiny invisible vibrating wiggly lines
My blood turns into ink
Despair can help accomplish many things
Work with the worst you can think

Tiny invisible vibrating wiggly lines
Dance across the air
Scream if you care
Honk if you're horny
Smile while it's still free

Expose yourself on camera
Deceive with the guilty
Stand up for what you believe
A rare occasion sorrow generates
Somewhere in the grey
The perfection of opposite extremes
Good and evil become the same

Watching the sun come up
The inspiring beautiful sight
But we witness it all too often
What keeps you up all night

So go on and suffer through your tragedy
Everyone gets their share
Of the fuel that fires creative expression
Dancing across the air

Stupid Get Angry

When the going gets tough
The stupid get angry
I don't have time for infantile spite
Please stop yelling
You sound like you're crazy
I am not going to argue
Because you're always right

Guilt

You know its waiting for you
And it's going to fuck you up
It's going to make you broken
You have run out of luck

You feel it staring at you
Ready to take you down
And you know that you deserve it
Too late to change it now

It's coming for you – impending doom
Turn off all the lights – lock yourself in your room

You could have avoided this
But you pay no heed
Remember how you spoke too much
Remember those dirty deeds

This thing can ruin homes
It cancels dreams, tares flesh from bone
No great new lie can save you now
You should have changed your ways somehow

Transmissions

Here's another poem that may never get read
I'm just relaying a transmission
How do these words enter my head

Never a rhyme or reason
For a reason to rhyme
Prose from the dimensional void
An oblivious disregard for the hands of time

Turn your thoughts into art
Let your anger create
Just who or what is really in control
Of this manifesting state

Where do these words come from?
Unread poems or songs never sung
And when these transmissions eventually stop
I'm left to my own devices and I return to writer's block

So if this page makes it out of the pile
And you are reading along
Remember these are just words
That I picked out of the wind from the abysmal lexicon

Consume

Pick your poison and get to it
Smoke it, poke it, drink it or glue it
Don't listen to what others have to say
Just get fucked up and waste the day

Quit your job or get kicked out of school
Intoxication is the only rule
Ignore all those who tell you to abstain
Outlaw sobriety and brand the coherent insane

New Clown in Town

There's a…
New clown in town
A home to roam
His stash of cash
Pays first not last
Job for a slob
Day of first pay
Car to the bar
Ho with some blow
Stopped by the cops
Brought to the shop
Bail out of jail
Back to his shack
Calls down the hall
Cash for more stash
Night into light
Jerk misses work
Home on the phone
Plan with the man
Meet for that treat
High as the sky
Dough is running low
Pay gone in days
Spent all his rent
Slob lost his job
Car back to bar
Just one last glass
Insane pays with change

Life is just strife
New clown in town
Slice of the knife
Next day gone away

After The End

The sun goes black

All colour turns grey

Reality has packed up all of its belongings

And has gone on holiday

Your souls were always in direst jeopardy

Your mere existence is a con

So much for your faith, your gods and your afterlife

All religions have been proven wrong

And now everything is gone

Time no longer exists

Your entire life happened all at once, and then someone flicked a switch

Skeletons

I've introduced her to the skeletons in my closet

She knows where I've been, she has no fear

She's met the demons that haunt my past

And she alone was standing with me when all the smoke cleared

Mainstream

We will walk with the damned we will turn into salt
We will protect the guilty and live with their faults
We will march into hell with inherent clout
We will rise from the ashes if there is a way out
We will butcher the innocent and make them not so
We will take blame for thrown rocks
Because rocks we will throw
We will destroy the average if we do have our way
We are pissing in the mainstream
We won't swim there these days

Lost

Exhausted and full of despair
Sickly and bloated, eyes full of hair
Breaking and broken, the unheard of spoken
Wearing out the night
A tragedy always in sight
One last smoke forever
Or until the morning comes
Put off what's important and go find some sun
Life on the run
Alone in the dark
The distant dog barks
Beckoning me home
To examine the options and search the unknown
I will not make it on my own
I cannot build this thing alone
I haven't the strength the carry the stone
So give me your hand, help me find my way home

Individuals

I have chosen not to be individual
I once thought of myself as a complete original
But I no longer have to be myself
For everyone becomes someone else

Anger

The poison in my head is the anger I have taken to bed
So I try to see clearly through the red
It's best to talk it over and leave nothing unsaid

Religion

Religion is hate
Religion is fear
Religion is ignorance
Religion is kill
Religion is blind
Religion is evil
Religion's pockets are always filled
Religion is suffering
Religion is death
Religion is a lie
Religion is war
Religion is greed
Religion is fraud
And religion just isn't needed anymore

Dementia

Suddenly conscious
Dark, alone, cold, there's nothing familiar
A million miles from home
Reduced capacity
Regressed scattered memories
Something out there begins to moan
The clock on the wall is threatening to kill you
Your skin feels alive, this is going to stay with you
You're running out of time
Somebody whispers "please don't die"
Glowing red eyes stare from the corner of your room
But there's nobody there, just a vision in the gloom
The twisted landscapes keep on changing
Your reality is re-arranging
The dark bad things are growing and gathering
Your last shred of sanity begins unravelling
Souls of the unwanted dead wander these halls
It's a wide open mind-fuck-free for all
You will never have peace
You will never be free
You are the usurper of your own cosmic scheme
And as you realize this dementia is no longer a dream
You not only accept, but embrace insanity

Doomed

He wills himself to come alive
He's on a path usually resisted
This ornamentally metaphoric edge to some never existed
The first day of the rest of his life
For the last time, born again once more
He keeps a close eye on reality
It's flipped a bitch on him before
His ever spiraling twisted mind
Keeps festering pain in the dark
From the memory of an atrocity
As a child left alone in a dimly lit park
He now appears out of his room
Into the gloom, tears in his eyes
Gripping his spoon
But nobody's there and no one would care
If he's close to his doom
Thick is the air
Glowing full moon
Too many lies
Desperation looms
Broke too many ties, due to the spoon
No time for goodbye
Could have been me
Could have been you

Temptation

You know you shouldn't do it; you thought about it
You know you shouldn't do it; you did it anyway
You know you shouldn't do it; you did it one more time
You know you shouldn't do it; now you do it every day

One Hell of a Storm

Like an atom bomb
Like when mountains fall
Then the downpour begins to blanket us all
That which falls to the ground belongs to the ground
Wrapped up in thunder
Immersed in the greatest of sound
It just keeps on raining
The rivers overflowing
Blackouts are occurring
The cruisers begin cruising
The thunder never stopping
The lightning bright and frightening
Did someone see this coming?
Why does it keep on raining?
Radio broadcast warning
Take shelter 'til the morning
The storm just keeps on storming
Could last 40 days straight
The puddles have turned into rivers
My neighbourhood has become a lake

Salvation

Help me to carry on
Let the tired wind blow me away
There is something waiting, maybe watching as well
I was soon to start counting my numbered days
But I have found this generous form of self-assurance
That may lead to my salvation
After all these years it's finally time
To start taking steps away from my damnation
Cosmic scheme on the phone
Relaying definitive proof
To believe you must understand
Creative success and the burden of self-destruction
Have always walked hand in hand

Succeed

The awful truth about our existence
The faults of mankind
What makes us so wrong
Destroy, rebuild
Divide and conquer
Those born in complacency will find somewhere to belong
The old dream was a big backyard
The more people there are, the more people there will be
Billions multiply, pave the countryside
Reality is a crooked lie
It's expensive to be free
There's just so much room for the healthy and wealthy
The rest of us sick and in need
What once was the greatest country in the world
The once middle class are now eating squirrel
They cut the poor, someone had to bleed
Work your whole life, the down payment's in need
Work your whole life, pay that mortgage
Work your whole life, they won't let you get rich
Work your whole life, or open your own crooked business
Fuck good people over, there's always church for forgiveness

Pride

There's an urgency that disrupts me
Some unknown force that pushes and pulls
It's led better men to madness
Makes a needy man believe he's full

Drunk

Your eyes are getting hazy
It's time for you to retire
You drank up every drop in sight
And you're completely wired
The devil made you do it
And you really had some fun
But you won't remember anything
You will blackout, way too spun
You're drunk, go to bed
Sleep the poison out of your head
Get up tomorrow do it all over again
It's the vicious circle that never ends
Go to bed you're drunk!

Mars

It's hard to say if the privileged would ever speak these words
The human race is a savage animal, the hypocrisy is absurd
There is blind optimism for the rest
Which does not affect me
Why do some believe in the unreal
When it seems plain for all to see
There's nothing for us out in space
Just scenery, are the stars
A dying dream for a fading race
No one will ever live on Mars
Sometimes the end seems near
Sometimes it's not too far
I believe we are to remain here forever
No one will ever live on Mars
I'm sure we're gonna die trying
But the place is just too far
Our future changes day to day
But we will never live on Mars

The Last

Dare to be brave and fearless
And high, it's not a disguise
Or is it, just wait?
What difference is straight
Would it all be the same
Would the strange somehow change
I don't think it will be
There is something I see
It's ugly but shines
With uneven lines
It's beautiful with spots
And goes over the top
So I'm going to push this envelope
I'm gonna do it fast
With the vow I'll always keep it real
Even if I finish last

Temptation II

It will follow you home like a lost starving puppy
It'll keep you up late and it leaves you wanting more
Then the next day, the smoke gets cleared away
And it's waiting again outside your door

Distress

I know you struggle with the weight of impending doom
I can see it in your eyes there's nowhere to hide
I can see the pressure coming down on you
The biggest mistakes always seem to come at the worst possible time
And your obvious pain reveals the truth
Stop declaring that you're fine

Dusty Underground Palace II

There is much more to be sacrificed
For the greater the dream, the higher the price
And it's proper to let young minds go to waste
It's how we prepare, those of us from this place
For we are not God's children
We are dirty, we are loud
And if we end up in hell for cause and belief
Then at least we will go to hell proud
You will have more to fear when you finally leave here
Although I am sure you won't
So stop doing the things that you do, but shouldn't
And start doing the things you should do, but don't

Peace

Who put the crown on top of the clown?
Foolish Kings will bring Kingdoms down
Amassing armies of human cattle
Both sides fight a losing battle
It's absurd, why do we still believe?
Peace through death can be achieved
I refuse to take sides in conflict anymore
My only fight will be against fighting war

Numb

Have you stayed up all night thinking
Can you paint out the blue
Have you got that sinking feeling
Why can't I get through
Are you concerned about the damage
Will you easily break
Is there a mutual misunderstanding
Or just my mistake

Unheard

Never follow the evil ways of this world
Give to society what it offers you back
I've got more than one reason for rebellion
Something that the unheard must lack

Generation Gap

The youth are unbalanced
So they plan a devious atrocity
Troubles of tomorrow are mounting
The children play rough in the hard summer heat
It draws them in to a poisonous fountain
But what a cruel harsh world
Razor in the apple and cut the break line
A drastic measure to eliminate the young
And ensure the rest of us survive
The kids are all fucked up
We must remove this generation
Give Mother Nature a little rest
And let time heal the situation

Goodbye

This goes out to our dearly departed
One last collective goodbye
We raise a glass for those who have passed
Long before their time
Another friend has left us
Once again, it's just not fair
So this is for the memories
And everything we shared
So long old friend is the message we send
We raise our glasses high
Goodbye old friend will we see you again?
Somewhere on the great other side
It's the unexpected tragedy
That leaves us numb and scared
So once again for the memory
Once again for all we shared

Approaching the End

I've been staring at the sky
I've lost all sense of time
Have I been touched by the light
Or am I losing my mind
Point me to the divine
Show me another sign
From the other side
Is this the end of the line
I now eagerly await all incoming transmissions
The sender was once unknown
I was starting to believe I had been touched by God
But now He calls me on the phone
You won't believe what He said
There are millions about to die
He didn't say how, He didn't say why
But it's too late to pick a side
That's what He said
Millions soon to be dead
So break your last bread
Take your last med
We are approaching the end

The last one in the book

Writing about it doesn't help anymore
So this is the last chapter
This will be the final score
I will then be silenced
To urge dissent no more
And then I will turn inward
Find something new to explore

I feel that something's got to break
What small detail will be the big mistake?

What I have been saying has been said before
In many different ways
By those who sleep on floors

I've watched it all go wrong
Few heed warnings that most of us ignore
So I ask the masses someone please speak for me
Please don't give up the struggle
Don't give up this war

www.ingramcontent.com/pod-product-compliance
Lightning Source LLC
LaVergne TN
LVHW092023190726
843493LV00002B/556